Revised Comprehensive Conservation Plan

*Koyukuk/Northern Unit Innoko/Nowitna
National Wildlife Refuges*

DECISION SUMMARY

September 2009

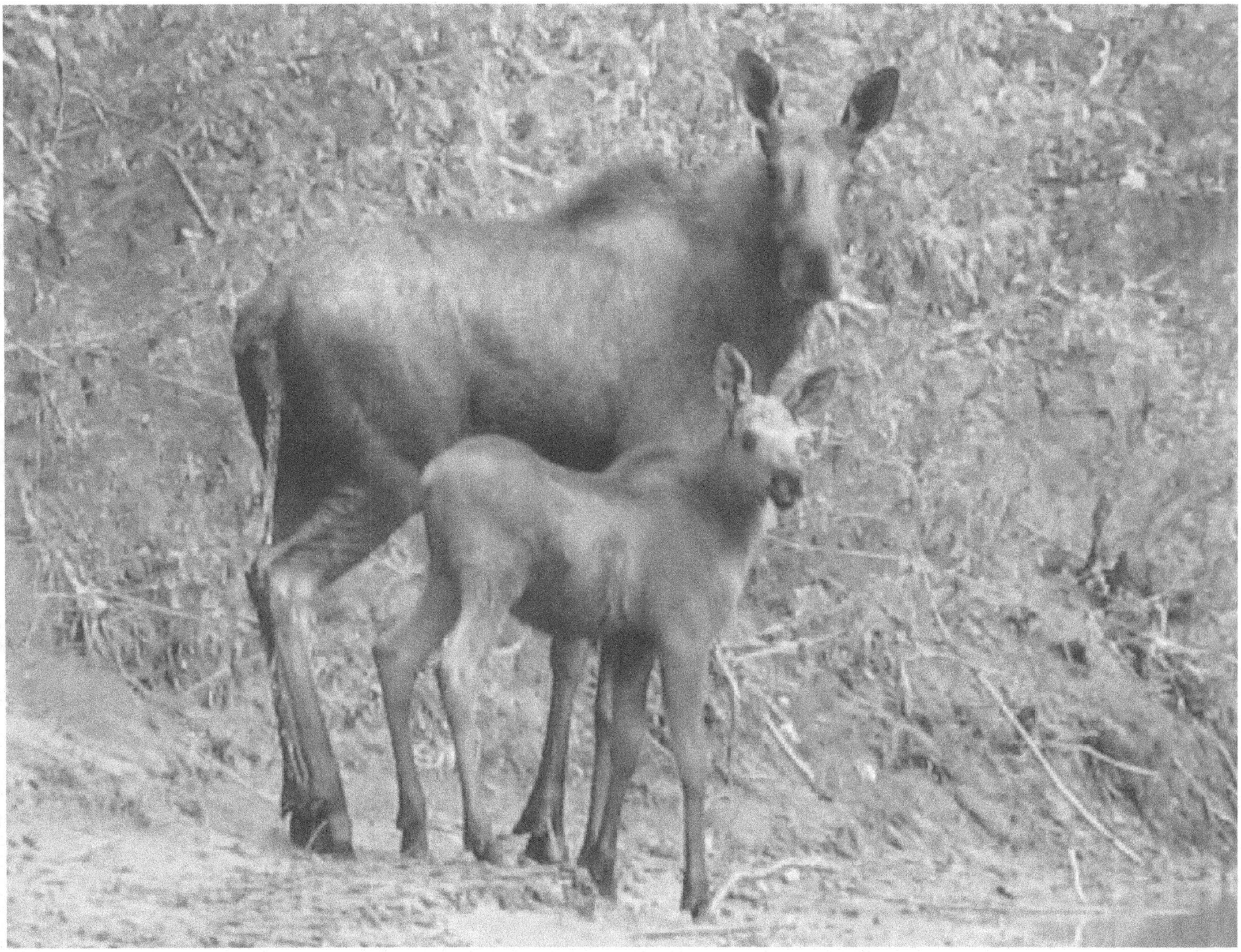

U.S. Fish and Wildlife Service Mission Statement

The mission of the U.S. Fish and Wildlife Service is working with others to conserve, protect, and enhance fish, wildlife, plants, and their habitats for the continuing benefit of the American people.

National Wildlife Refuge System Mission Statement

The mission of the National Wildlife Refuge System is to administer a national network of lands and waters for the conservation, management, and where appropriate, restoration of the fish, wildlife, and plant resources and their habitats within the United States for the benefit of present and future generations of Americans.

National Wildlife Refuge System Improvement Act of 1997

Introduction to the Comprehensive Conservation Plan

A revised and updated Draft Comprehensive Conservation Plan for Koyukuk, Northern Unit Innoko, and Nowitna National Wildlife Refuges (Refuge) was completed in the summer of 2008. In March 2009 Regional Director Geoffrey L. Haskett signed the Finding of No Significant Impact (FONSI) adopting the Service's preferred alternative (Alternative B) as described in the Revised Comprehensive Conservation Plan for the Koyukuk/ Northern Unit Innoko/Nowitna National Wildlife Refuges (Revised Conservation Plan). The adopted Conservation Plan reflects the U. S. Fish and Wildlife Service's (Service) intent to manage the Refuge to achieve the mission of the Service and the National Wildlife Refuge System (System) and meet the purposes for which the Refuge was established, in settings that emphasize natural, unaltered landscapes. Implementation of the Revised Conservation Plan began with signing of the FONSI.

The Koyukuk River meanders through its namesake Refuge before joining the Yukon River next to the community of Koyukuk.

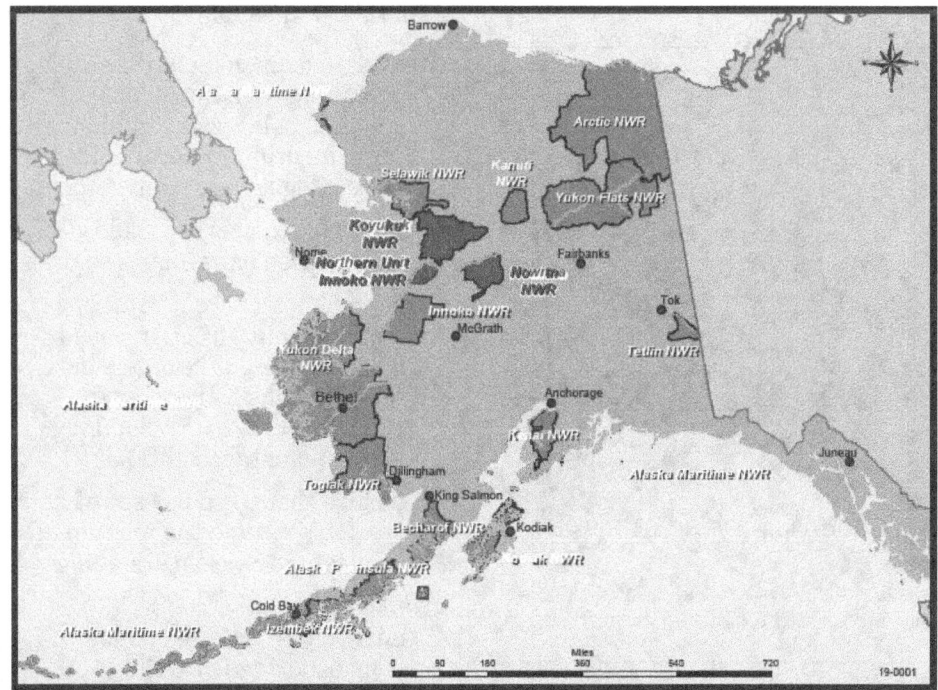

Refuge locations. The Northern Unit Innoko Refuge is locally known as Kaiyuh Flats.

Boney Creek dissects the Benchlands on the Nowitna Refuge.

What are Conservation Plans?

A Conservation Plan provides broad policy guidance and establishes overall refuge management direction. They ensure that management actions and refuge uses comply with the purposes for which a refuge was established and with other legal mandates. They define long-term goals and objectives toward which refuge management activities will be directed for the next 15 years and provide opportunities for public involvement.

The Kaiyuh Flats consist of a mosaic of wetlands, non-forested upland habitat with a mixture of low shrubs and grass, and conifer and deciduous forests.

Purpose and Need for Plan Revision

The Alaska National Interest Lands Conservation Act (ANILCA) of 1980, as amended, directs the Service to "prepare and, from time to time, revise, a comprehensive conservation plan for each refuge" in Alaska. The Revised Conservation Plan updates and replaces the management direction from the 1987 Conservation Plans for the Refuges.

The purpose of the Revised Conservation Plan is to ensure activities, actions, and management fulfill the purposes for which the Refuges were established and to provide clear direction to the public and refuge staff on how the Service intends to meet those purposes. While the 1987 Conservation Plans have provided good general direction, we needed to update and revise them to reflect changes in our understanding of the resources and uses on the Refuges, and changes in laws, regulations, and policies affecting refuge management that have occurred since the 1987 Conservation Plans were developed. We also combined the original plans into a single plan which covers all three refuge units, and more accurately reflects refuge management.

Gravel bar along the Nowitna River. The lower 223 miles of the Nowitna River is managed as a Wild River under the Wild and Scenic Rivers Act.

The calm waters of Dulbi River with its reflections impart a sense of serenity.

The wetlands of the Kaiyuh Flats provide excellent breeding habitat for thousands of waterfowl.

Revising the 1987 Conservation Plans allowed us to:

- update management direction according to national and regional policies and guidelines implementing Federal laws governing refuge management;

- incorporate new scientific information on refuge resources;

- re-evaluate current refuge management direction based on changing public demands for use of the Refuges and their resources, and changing environmental conditions;

- ensure that the purposes of the Refuges and the mission of the Refuge System are being fulfilled;

- ensure that national policy is incorporated into the management of the Refuges;

- ensure that all interested parties have an opportunity to participate in the development of management direction;

- provide a systematic process for making and documenting decisions about refuge resources;

- establish broad management direction for refuge programs and activities;

- provide continuity in refuge management;

- provide a basis for budget and personnel requests; and

- provide a basis for evaluating accomplishments.

Establishment of the Refuge

In 1980, President Jimmy Carter signed the Alaska National Interest Lands Conservation Act (ANILCA or Act) into law. The Act, among other things, established Koyukuk, Northern Unit Innoko, and Nowitna National Wildlife Refuges and identified their purposes. The Act states that the purposes of the Refuges include—

(i) (Koyukuk Refuge) to conserve the fish and wildlife populations and habitats in their natural diversity including, but not limited to, waterfowl and other migratory birds, moose, caribou (including participation in coordinated ecological studies and management of the Western Arctic caribou herd), furbearers, and salmon;

(i) (Innoko Refuge) to conserve fish and wildlife populations and habitats in their natural diversity including, but not limited to, waterfowl, peregrine falcons, other migratory birds, black bear, moose, furbearers, and other mammals and salmon;

(i) (Nowitna Refuge) to conserve fish and wildlife populations and habitats in their natural diversity including, but not limited to, trumpeter swans, white-fronted geese, canvasbacks and other waterfowl and migratory birds, moose, caribou, martens, wolverines and other furbearers, salmon, sheefish, and northern pike;

(ii) to fulfill the international treaty obligations of the United States with respect to fish and wildlife and their habitats;

(iii) to provide, in a manner consistent with the purposes set forth in subparagraphs (i) and (ii), the opportunity for continued subsistence uses by local residents;

(iv) to ensure, to the maximum extent practicable and in a manner consistent with the purposes set forth in paragraph (i), water quality and necessary water quantity within the refuge.

The purpose of the 400,000-acre **Koyukuk Wilderness** is to secure an enduring resource of wilderness, to protect and preserve the wilderness character of the area as part of the National Wilderness Preservation System, and to administer the area for the use and enjoyment of the American people in a way that will leave it unimpaired for future use and enjoyment as wilderness.

The lower 223 miles of the **Nowitna River** is managed as a **Wild River** under the Wild and Scenic Rivers Act. This segment of the river was recognized for its outstandingly remarkable scenic, geologic, wildlife, historic, and recreational values. There are 142,400 acres that fall under this management category. 🐾

Peregrine falcons usually nest on cliff edges. They belong to the fastest animals in the world, reaching up to 200 mph in a dive for prey.

Steve Emmons/USFWS

A bull moose drops its antlers in the fall and regrows them in the spring. It takes three to five months for the antlers to comletely regrow.

Melanie Hans/USFWS

Marten are curious critters and like to investigate.

Melanie Hans/USFWS

Lesser Canada geese feeding on shore.

Melanie Hans/USFWS

Fall colors along the Nowitna River.

Rising mist on a cool autumn morning.

Refuge Vision

The National Wildlife Refuges in the Koyukon region of Alaska encompass a vast area of boreal forest, wetlands, lakes, and rivers that is home to an abundance of waterfowl, songbirds, mammals, and fish. An experience of solitude in this intact ecosystem imparts the sense that this place is completely untouched by man. And yet, the land is thoroughly known and essential to people whose lives are intertwined with its bounty. We use our understanding of the respect, value and love of this place by the people who live in, use, or simply treasure this wild land and sound biological research and monitoring to ensure proper stewardship of the Koyukuk, Northern Unit Innoko, and Nowitna National Wildlife Refuges.

Reflections of the Dulbi River on Koyukuk Refuge.

Three-Day Slough on the Koyukuk Refuge. Winter in Interior Alaska lasts approximately eight months. During this time, the land is dominated by snow, ice, and often severe cold.

Goals and Objectives

The vision statement and refuge purposes provide the framework for developing management goals and objectives. Goals are broad statements of desired future conditions. Objectives are concise statements of what the Refuges want to accomplish. The planning team developed twelve management goals; several objectives were identified for each goal. Some objectives, though identified under a specific goal, may apply to more than one goal. When appropriate, objectives will be carried out in coordination with the Alaska Department of Fish and Game, other State and Federal agencies, and other cooperators.

Identified as an important issue to be addressed in the plan, **climate change** is specifically and implicitly related to many of the refuge objectives. See Goal 1, Objectives 1 and 4 in particular (Section 2.1.1 of the Revised Conservation Plan). The updated Inventory and Monitoring Plan (I&MP) will incorporate new studies and projects focused on climate change, and will recommend continuing cooperation with educational institutions, federal and State agencies, tribal organizations, and others to develop and implement research on global climate change and incorporate new monitoring efforts into the I&MP.

Goal 1: Fish and Wildlife. Conserve fish and wildlife populations and habitats in their natural diversity in a manner consistent with natural ecological processes.

Objectives include:

- Continue to implement and update the current Inventory and Monitoring Plan—reflecting changes in techniques; focus new projects on invasive species, climate change, water quality, and wetlands; and including new and ongoing cooperative efforts.

- Continue to work cooperatively with others to identify key fisheries resources and to fill in gaps in the Refuges' knowledge of fisheries resources; develop and implement research on effects of climate change on refuge resources; and incorporate new monitoring efforts that focus on detecting long-term changes to refuge ecosystems.

- Upon funding, hire a fisheries biologist/hydrologist and a wildlife biologist.

Refuge biologist watching for birds during the annual breeding bird survey.

Refuge pilot installing high-visibility snow marker to measure snow depth through the winter months.

Refuge biologist catching tadpoles and frogs to check for deformities.

Refuge biologist banding a greater white-fronted goose.

Chinook (King) salmon run up rivers and creeks in all three refuges.

Forest fires...

...and flooding are the main ecological drivers of Interior Alaska Refuges.

Goal 2: Ecosystem Health. Ensure the natural character, vigor, and species diversity of the boreal forest and tundra environments by perpetuating a fire regime both natural and prescribed, which maintains a mosaic of habitats native to Interior Alaska.

Objectives include:

- Continue to implement the Refuges' Fire Management and Communication plans

- Continue to refine our understanding of the refuge fire history by maintaining and incorporating the most current information into the geographic information system data base.

Goal 3: Fire Management. Maintain a fire management program that helps achieve Refuge goals and objectives while providing for the protection of human life, private property, and identified cultural and natural resources.

Objectives include:

- Combine the Koyukuk, Nowitna, and Northern Unit Innoko fire management plans into a single updated plan, incorporating changes resulting from the revised Conservation Plan along with current policy.

- Continue to contact tribal and local governments in villages near the Refuges to assess hazardous fuel reduction needs and develop a mitigation and monitoring plan.

- Update the Refuges' geographic information system coverage of cultural resource values at risk and other fire-related information.

- Continue to develop partnerships with other federal and State agencies and local governments to further the understanding of fire interactions in Interior Alaska.

- Upon funding, hire an assistant fire management officer.

Forest fire on the Kaiyuh Flats.

Goal 4: Water Resources. Ensure the natural function and condition of water resources necessary to conserve fish and wildlife populations and habitats in their natural diversity.

Objectives include:

- Develop, with assistance from the Service's Water Resources Branch or other partners, inventory and monitoring programs for refuge wetland, river, and stream resources, focusing on aquatic plants, fish and wildlife, aquatic invertebrates, and physical and chemical properties of wetlands, lakes, rivers, and streams.

- Review and evaluate the Refuges' 1986-1988 baseline evaluation of placer mining sedimentation and occurrence of heavy metals on associated aquatic resources; develop and implement a repeat survey.

Goal 5: Communication. Provide information and maintain open communication for a greater understanding and appreciation of fish and wildlife ecology, habitat preservation, and refuge management that assists in addressing resource issues important to local residents, the Service, and others.

Objectives include:

- Conduct school programs and community meetings on a regular basis; utilize other communication tools (informational kiosks, displays, radio programs, newsletters, brochures, and web sites) to provide timely and accurate information about refuge resources and programs to the public.

- Maintain the existing refuge resource library and continue working with local schools to develop resources for environmental education.

- Maintain partnerships with the Galena City Schools and the Louden Tribal Council to annually conduct the Galena Science Camp.

- Increase cooperation with the Friends of Alaska National Wildlife Refuges, particularly with their local representatives, to develop new materials and outlets for interpretation and environmental education.

Damselfly larvae live in the water and pray on mosquitoes and other small invertebrates.

Water Lily.

Children discovering wetlands during the Galena Science Camp.

Friends of Alaska National Wildlife Refuges is an independent, non-profit 501(c)(3) organization dedicated to promoting the conservation of the natural resources of all the Alaska National Wildlife Refuges.

Goal 6: Outdoor Recreation. Continue to provide opportunities for hunting, fishing, wildlife observation and photography, and other outdoor recreation in a natural setting.

Objectives include:

- Review current public use monitoring methods; implement new methodologies, if needed. Continue to assess levels of public use based on data from the Koyukuk River and Nowitna River hunter check stations and refuge guide and air taxi reports.

- Continue to develop the refuge law enforcement program, in conjunction with local communities and State and federal authorities, through activities such as hunter education, village visits, aerial surveillance, and annual special use permit reviews.

The rivers on the Refuges attract canoeists seeking solitude and adventure.

USFWS

Gravel bars along the rivers—here along the upper Nowitna—make for excellent camping spots.

Karin Lehmkuhl Bodony/USFWS

The Refuges provide outstanding opportunities for wildlife observation.

Deborah Webb/USFWS

Many areas on the Refuges are only accessible by air taxis equipped with floats.

USFWS

By annually maintaining a hunter check station at the mouth of the Nowitna River, refuge staff keep track of the number of moose harvested on the Refuge.

USFWS

Goal 7: Subsistence. Provide and promote the opportunity for local residents to continue their subsistence activities on the Refuge, consistent with the subsistence priority and with other refuge purposes.

Objectives include:

- Continue the Refuge Information Technician (RIT) program to enhance local information exchange; seek funding to restore the second RIT position.

- Continue to conduct annual informational meetings on the refuge biological program in local villages; work closely with tribal councils and other local, regional, State, and Federal working groups, committees, and councils to address issues and concerns of local subsistence users.

- Continue coordination and assistance with Migratory Bird Harvest Surveys and In-Season Fish Harvest Surveys (Yukon River Drainage Fisheries Association).

- Cooperate with village organizations and other agencies to develop opportunities to educate local youth and adults in traditional subsistence ways; continue to develop outreach tools that make subsistence regulations understandable to the public.

- Monitor and assess the use of off-road vehicles on refuge lands by federally qualified subsistence users and produce a report that determines if ORVs were traditionally used for subsistence access and examines the need for regulation of their use.

Three-Day Slough on the Koyukuk Refuge is one of the most productive areas for moose. Moose are an important subsistence resource for people living in local communities.

Freshly caught Chinook (King) salmon. King salmon is one of the major food staples for people living on and near the Refuges.

Salmon are often caught by using drift nets. .

Chum (Dog) salmon is sometimes used to feed sled dogs.

Refuge staff member measuring antlers of a harvested moose.

Chum salmon drying on racks.

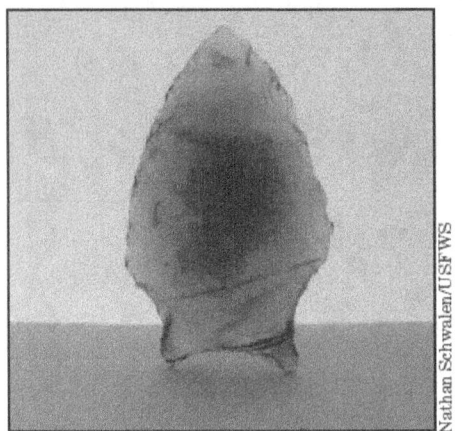

In 2001, Obsidian artifacts were found on the Koyukuk Refuge.

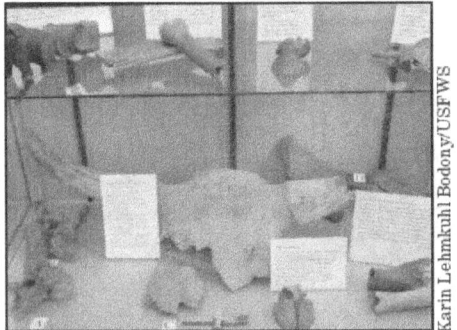

Galena City hall display of pleistocene bones found on the Refuges.

The Nowitna River Canyon within the Wild River section is considered a particularly scenic stretch of the river.

Aerial view of the Nogabahara Sand Dunes in the middle of the boreal forest.

Goal 8: Wild Character. Maintain the special values of the Nowitna Wild River and Koyukuk Wilderness and the wild character of the Refuge.

Objectives:

• Continue to monitor activities on the Nowitna Wild River and Koyukuk Wilderness for compliance with the Wild and Scenic Rivers and Wilderness acts and ANILCA; take appropriate action if non-compliance is identified.

Goal 9: Cultural Resources. Conserve, appreciate, and interpret the cultural, historic and prehistoric resources of the Refuge.

Objectives include:

• Prepare a Cultural Resources Management Guide for the Refuges.

• Provide training on the Archaeological Resources Protection Act and the National Historic Preservation Act to refuge employees.

• Identify and monitor all cultural sites at risk from vandalism and erosion; identify priority areas to inventory.

• Work with local tribes, elders, universities, museums, other partners, and the regional archaeological staff to: compile a place names directory and atlas of cultural and historic sites; develop an active bibliography and library collection of published and unpublished materials related to cultural, paleontological, and natural history of the Refuges; investigate and evaluate known cultural sites and identify new sites in the Refuges; and explore the unique paleontological resources of the Nowitna Refuge.

• Cooperate with tribes, local residents, and others to develop and enhance programs that capture traditional knowledge about the cultural and natural history of the Refuges.

The Nogabahara Sand Dunes cover about 16,000 acres and are within the Koyukuk Wilderness. The individual dunes can be 50 to 200 feet high and up to 300 feet long.

Goal 10: Cooperation with partners. Promote close working relationships through effective coordination, interaction, and cooperation with other federal agencies, State agencies, local communities, tribes, organizations, industries, the general public, and the landowners within and adjacent to the Refuge whose programs relate to Refuge management activities.

Objective:

- Collaborate with other refuges, federal and State agencies, research institutions, schools, tribal and city councils, and others to facilitate resource management, inventory and monitoring, biological research, public outreach, and education at the Refuges and in the region.

A presentation about climate change by refuge staff in Huslia.

Goal 11: Facilities and Equipment. Provide and maintain adequate facilities and equipment in Galena to ensure a safe and secure working environment to accomplish Refuge purposes, goals, and mandates.

Objectives:

- Fund construction or purchase of an administrative office, shop, and warehouse in Galena.

- Maintain and upgrade the quarters, bunkhouse, and administrative cabins to accommodate employees in subarctic conditions; continue exploring alternative energy sources for refuge facilities.

- Explore options and funding to acquire an adequate float plane facility and operations site on Alexander Lake in Galena.

A sled dog team passing through Galena on its way to Nome during the Iditarod. Refuge headquarters are in the background.

Goal 12: Staffing. Ensure the Refuge has adequate personnel to meet operational needs.

Objectives:

- Restore funding for a wildlife biologist position and second RIT position; seek funding to hire an additional biological technician. Create and seek funding for a fisheries biologist/hydrologist position and an assistant fire management officer.

- Work with regional high schools and universities in recruiting and educating diverse candidates for refuge positions.

- Maintain a minimum of three pilots on staff; add staff with pilot credentials as biological, habitat, and fisheries positions are funded. 🐾

The Hog River cabin, one of three administrative cabins owned by the Refuges.

Refuge biologists fit moose with radio collars to gain a better understanding of mortality and movement.

Much of the work requires access to remote areas by float plane.

The Revised Conservation Plan

Management direction under the Revised Conservation Plan will generally continue to follow the same course of action as under the 1987 conservation plan as modified in subsequent step-down management plans (e.g., fisheries and fire management plans, cultural resources management guide). The new vision statement and the goals and objectives developed by the refuge staff will be incorporated into the management direction for the Refuge. Regional management policies and guidelines, as modified for the Refuge, will be incorporated.

Regional Management Policies and Guidelines

Management of refuges in Alaska is governed by federal laws including the National Wildlife Refuge System Administration Act and ANILCA, regulations implementing these laws, treaties, U.S. Fish and Wildlife Service policy, and principles of sound resource management. All of these establish standards for resource management, and may address the range of potential activities that may be allowed on refuges. Management policies and guidelines described in the plan were developed for national wildlife refuges in the Alaska Region. These policies and guidelines are essentially the same for all of the refuges in this region.

Land Management Categories

The Alaska National Interest Lands Conservation Act (ANILCA) requires us to designate areas according to their resources and values and to specify programs and uses within those areas. To meet this requirement, Minimal, Moderate, and Intensive management categories were established as part of the Service's Alaska-wide planning effort. Permissible uses of designated Wilderness areas and Wild and Scenic Rivers are subject to the Wilderness and Wild and Scenic Rivers acts and ANILCA.

Under the Revised Conservation Plan, refuge lands will continue to be managed in only three management categories as in the 1987 Conservation Plans. Of the 6,044,478 acres of federal land, about 5,502,078 acres are classified as Minimal Management, about 142,400 acres are classified as Wild River, and about 400,000 acres are classified as designated Wilderness. Selected lands (an additional 348,499 acres of land within the external boundaries of the Refuges) have yet to be conveyed and will be managed under the same management category as surrounding refuge lands until conveyed (or if the selection is denied). Appropriate activities, public uses, commercial uses, and facilities are identified in the plan for each management category. The table on the next two pages includes some of these uses. 🐾

Frosted leaves after a cold autumn night.

Fireweed gets its name from its brilliant color and from its ability to quickly recolonize areas burnt by forest fires.

Black spruce in the boreal forest of the Koyukuk Refuge in mid-winter.

Frosted willow bush along the Yukon River.

MANAGEMENT CATEGORIES

Minimal Management	5,502,078 acres (91% of total)
Wild River	142,400 acres (2% of total)
Designated Wilderness	400,000 acres (7% of total)

SPECIFIC MANAGEMENT DIRECTION

Ecosystem, Habitat, and Fish and Wildlife Management

Ecosystem and Landscape Management

Habitat Management – Prescribed Fire	May be allowed in Wilderness Management (will require a minimum requirements analysis). Allowed in Minimal and Wild River Management.

Fish and Wildlife Population Management

Fish and Wildlife Control – Chemical Habitat Modifications.	May be allowed in all management categories. Wilderness Management will require a minimum requirements analysis.

Access

Snowmobiles	Permitted for traditional activities, on or off designated trails, in period of adequate snow cover and on ice-covered rivers, subject to reasonable regulation.
Off-Road Vehicles (All-Terrain Vehicles) – Includes air boats and air cushion vehicles.	Not allowed (with very few exceptions).

Public Use, Recreation, and Outreach Activities

Administrative Facilities

Administrative Field Sites – Permanent facilities.	Use of existing sites allowed including replacement of existing facilities as necessary; new sites may be allowed in Wild River and Minimal Management. Wilderness Management will require a minimum requirements analysis.

Public Use and Recreation Facilities

Boat Launches and Docks – Designated sites for launching and storing watercraft or tying up a float plane.	May be allowed. Wilderness Management will require a minimum requirements analysis.
Visitor Contact Facilities – A variety of staffed and unstaffed facilities providing information on the Refuges and their resources to the public; facilities range from visitor centers to kiosks and signs.	May be allowed under Minimal and Wild River Management categories; generally not allowed in Wilderness.

Temporary Facilities – Includes tent frames, caches, and other similar or related facilities; does not include gravel pads for tents, hardened trails, and/or primitive toilets.	Tent platforms may be authorized by permit. All others may be allowed in Wilderness, Wild River, and Minimal Management categories.

Commercial Uses

Other Commercial Activities

Transportation and Utility Systems – Includes transmission lines, pipeline, telephone and electrical power lines, oil and gas pipelines, communications systems, roads, airstrips, and other necessary related facilities. Does not include facilities associated with on-refuge oil and gas development.	Must be authorized by Congress under Wilderness Management; may be authorized under Wild River Management and Minimal Management categories but will require a plan amendment.

Staffing and Budget Needs

	Short-Term	Long-Term
Permanent Full-Time Employees	13	16
Permanent Seasonal Employees	1	3
Temporary Seasonal Employees	4	4
Volunteers	3-5	3-5
Total Annual Budget Needs	$2-2.4	$2.4-2.8

Cow moose and calf resting along the Dulbi River on the Koyukuk Refuge.

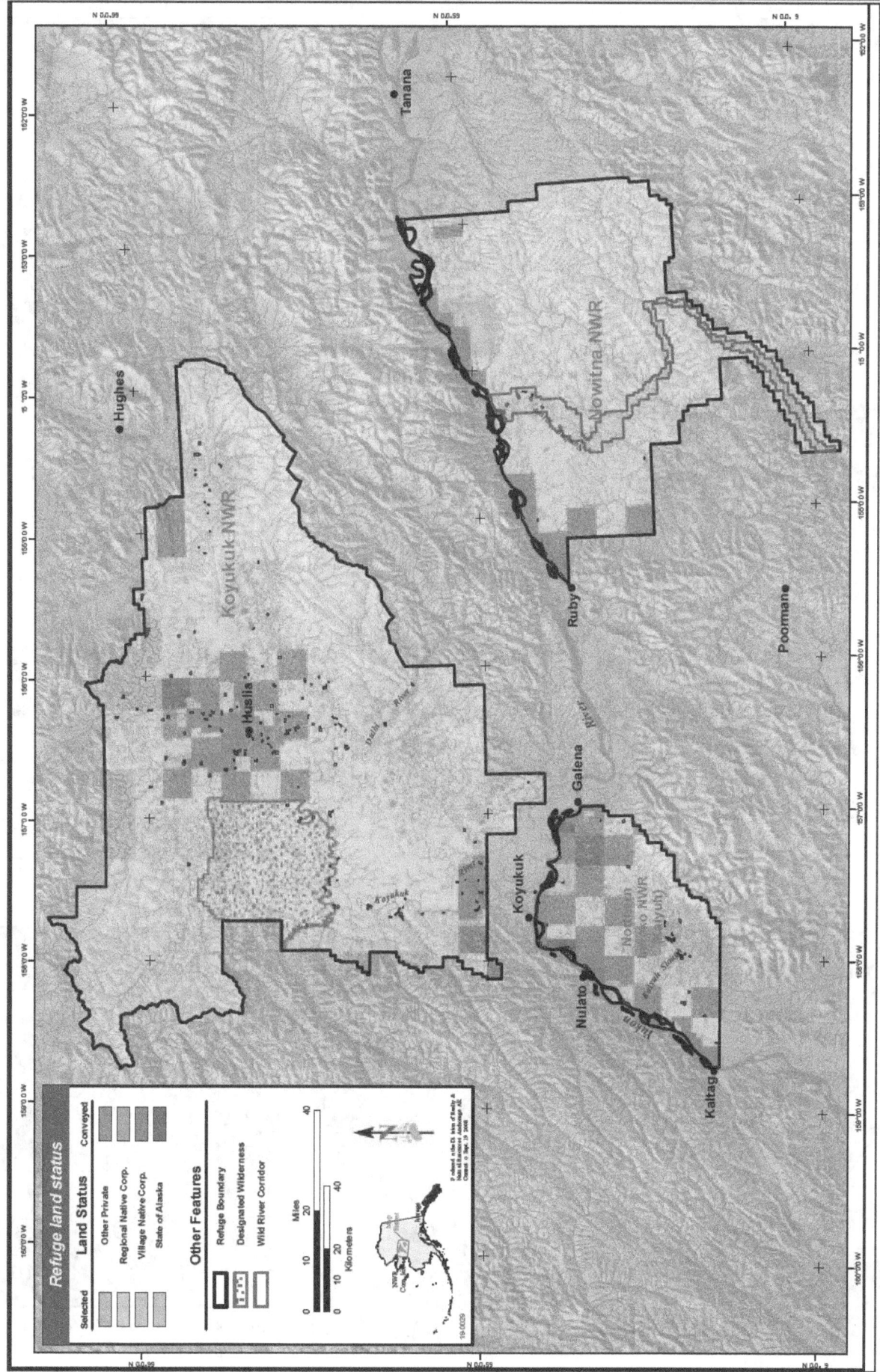

All federally owned land within the Refuges is in the Minimal Management category unless noted as Designated Wilderness or Wild River Corridor.

Implementation

Implementation of the Koyukuk/Northern Unit Innoko/Nowitna Refuges Revised Conservation Plan will be accomplished, in part, through development and implementation of various step-down plans. Each step-down plan has its own program focus (e.g., wildlife inventory and monitoring, fisheries management, fire management, visitor services), identifying and directing the implementation of strategies (actions, techniques, and tools) designed to achieve programmatic objectives outlined in the Conservation Plan (see Goals and Objectives previously in this document).

Another aspect of the implementation process includes identifying partnership opportunities (e.g., with Native organizations, the State of Alaska, local communities, other federal agencies, universities and museums, nongovernmental organizations, and other appropriate entities) that result in implementing strategies and accomplishing refuge objectives.

Greater white-fronted geese, also called speckle bellies.

Steve Emmons/USFWS

Both trumpeter and tundra swans occur on the Koyukuk Refuge. They look alike, but the trumpeter swan is larger and its bill is uniformly black as can be seen here, while the tundra swan's bill shows some yellow right underneath the eyes.

USFWS

Great-horned owl on the Kaiyuh Flats.

Melanie Hans/USFWS

Wing display of the common loon.

Jenny Bryant/USFWS

Male pine grosbeak; the female's plumage is gray with yellow-orange coloring on head, neck, and back.

Karin Lehmkuhl Bodony/USFWS

Approximately 78 citizens live in the community of Hughes northeast of the Koyukuk Refuge.

Ruby, an old mining town, lies nestled between the hills bordering the Nowitna Refuge.

Nulato—old town site. Several communities situated along rivers in Interior Alaska moved newer buildings onto higher ground to avoid the risk of flooding, resulting in an old town site and a new town site.

The city of Galena—new site.

Partnerships

Partnerships with other organizations are among the ways in which the Service fulfills its mission: "Working with others to conserve, protect and enhance fish, wildlife, and plants and their habitats for the continuing benefit of the American people."

The Refuges exist within a dynamic ecosystem. Many of the resources within the Refuges are of national and international importance. The Service recognizes that the public, various organizations, and other governmental agencies have interests in Refuges. Implementation of many refuge programs requires community involvement, support, and assistance.

The refuge staff looks for opportunities to coordinate activities with the following (among others):

- State of Alaska

- Other federal agencies

- Federal Subsistence Western Interior Regional Advisory Council

- Migratory Bird Co-management Council

- Tribal governments in Galena, Hughes, Huslia, Kaltag, Koyukuk, Nulato, Ruby, and Tanana

- Village corporations—Gana-A'Yoo (Galena, Koyukuk, Nulato, and Kaltag); K'oyitl'ots'ina, Limited (Hughes and Huslia); Dineega (Ruby); and Tozitna, Limited (Tanana)

- Tanana Chiefs Conference, Inc. (regional Native non-profit organization)

- Local governments in Galena, Hughes, Huslia, Kaltag, Koyukuk, Nulato, Ruby, and Tanana

- Yukon Koyukuk, City of Galena, and Tanana school districts

- Universities and museums

- Nongovernmental organizations (e.g., Friends of Alaska National Wildlife Refuges, Alaska Geographic, and Ducks Unlimited)

The community of Huslia is situated along the Koyukuk River at the center of the Koyukuk Refuge.

Monitoring and Evaluation

Monitoring and Evaluation: Monitoring helps the refuge staff track the progress of plan implementation. It is accomplished by a variety of methods, including surveys, inventories, and censuses. Table 4-1 in the Revised Conservation Plan (USFWS 2009; posted on the FWS website at http://alaska.fws.gov/nwr/planning/koynowpol.htm and on the web sites for Koyukuk and Nowitna refuges) includes more specific details on what monitoring questions the Refuge will ask and how they will evaluate their findings (key indicators, management standards, and possible management actions if standards are not being met). Proposed monitoring will be refined as wildlife and habitat inventory and monitoring, fisheries management, visitor services, and other step-down plans are prepared or revised. The results of monitoring show how refuge objectives are being achieved and help measure progress towards accomplishing refuge goals. Evaluation of these results may lead to amendment or revision of the Revised Conservation Plan. Such changes are a necessary part of the Service's adaptive management approach.

Black bear along the Nowitna River.

Bank swallows nest in colonies along the Dulbi River.

Rare sighting of a wolverine.

Mink (pictured) and otter look similar but the otter is much larger and has a flatter tail.

Caribou from the Galena Mountain herd.

Porcupine on the Nowitna Refuge.

Plan Amendment and Revision

Periodic review and change of this conservation plan will be necessary. As knowledge of refuge resources, users, and uses improves, changes in management may be identified. Fish and wildlife populations, user groups, adjacent land owners and users, and other management considerations change with time, often in unforeseen ways. Challenges also may be encountered in trying to implement the plan.

Revisions are a necessary part of the adaptive management approach used by the Service. This means that objectives and strategies to reach goals can be adjusted. Most of the resulting changes will fine-tune the plan. These changes will not require modification of this document because minor changes will be addressed in the more detailed refuge step-down and annual work plans. Only if a major change is required in management of the Refuges will it be necessary to revise this Conservation Plan with a new environmental document outside the regular review schedule.

To enable refuge users; adjacent landowners; local, state, and federal agencies; and other interested parties to express their views on how the Refuges are being managed, the Refuges will periodically hold meetings or use other techniques such as comment cards and surveys to solicit comments for evaluation purposes. By encouraging continuing public input, the Refuges will be better able to serve the public, to determine potential problems before they occur, and to take immediate action to resolve existing problems.

Every three to five years, refuge staff will review public comments, local and state government recommendations, staff recommendations, research studies, and other sources to determine if revisions to the plan are necessary. If major changes are proposed, public meetings may be held, and a new environmental assessment or environmental impact statement may be necessary. Full review and updating of the conservation plan will occur every 15 years.

Frozen Lake on the Nowitna Refuge.

USFWS

Sunset above Nowitna Refuge.

USFWS

Melanie Hans/USFWS

Reflections at the mouth of the Nowitna River.

**U. S. Department of the Interior
Fish and Wildlife Service
Region 7, Alaska**

FINDING OF NO SIGNIFICANT IMPACT

Revised Comprehensive Conservation Plan
Koyukuk and Northern Unit Innoko/Nowitna National Wildlife Refuge, Alaska

The U.S. Fish and Wildlife Service (Service) has completed the Revised Comprehensive Conservation Plan (Plan) for the Koyukuk and Northern Unit Innoko/Nowitna National Wildlife Refuge (Refuge). The draft revised plan and Environmental Assessment (EA) (herein incorporated by reference) describe two alternatives for managing the Refuge and associated effects on the human environment. No substantive changes in Alternative B, the proposed action, were made in response to public comments. Technical corrections and edits were made in response to public comments. Alternative B is selected for implementation.

Alternatives Considered

The Alaska National Interest Lands Conservation Act (ANILCA) requires the Service to designate areas according to their respective resources and values and to specify programs and uses. To meet this requirement, the Alaska Region established management categories for the refuges including Minimal, Moderate, Intensive, Wilderness, and Wild River Management. Appropriate activities, public uses, commercial uses, and facilities are identified for each management category. Minimal, Wilderness, and Wild River Management apply to the Refuge.

Two alternatives were considered in the EA. Alternative A, the no-action alternative, would continue current management. Alternative B, the proposed action, would include management direction updated by changes and adjustments to policy since completion of the 1987 plan. Alternative B also includes a vision statement, goals, and objectives for management of the Refuge. Under both alternatives, management of the refuge would generally continue to follow the current course of action, but Alternative B provides additional details in the vision statement, goals, and objectives and incorporates new regional management policies and guidelines. The distribution and amount of land in the Minimal, Wilderness, and Wild River Management is the same under both alternatives.

Public Review

Public comments on the draft plan and EA were solicited from October 6, 2008 through December 15, 2008. Public meetings were held in Galena, Hughes, Huslia, Kaltag, Koyukuk, Nulato, Ruby, and Tanana. These villages are located near or within the Refuge. Comments were received from four individuals, the State of Alaska; The Wilderness Society, the Nulato Tribal Council, and Born Free USA.

There were no comments specific to the draft plan received during the village meetings. The majority of comments made regarded the current population of moose, wolf, and salmon or wildlife observations made over the years.

One individual commenter asked "how about making these refuges into a wilderness area?" Another individual commented "that my priorities for our NWRs are making them places where animals and nature are prioritized, NOT humans and all their 'recreational' needs." The third individual said that "global warming is a great concern." A fourth individual, who commented via e-mail, felt we should use the word "protection" instead of "conservation"; hunting was not a compatible use; we are not meeting the needs of the public; there should be no prescribed fires; and old data was used for the analysis.

The state of Alaska made several helpful suggestions that clarified various parts of the plan. The Wilderness Society was concerned about the wilderness review process, wilderness stewardship and management, motorized and mechanized activities in wilderness, the wild and scenic river review process, and climate change. The Nulato Tribal Council was concerned about maintaining subsistence activities, an expired Land Bank Agreement, and the regulation of commercial guides, ATVs, and commercial timber harvest. Born Free USA was concerned about a comprehensive, biological inventory, management of trapping, the impacts of trapping and hunting, the use of leg-hold traps, and alternative trapping methods.

Revisions from Draft Plan

No substantive revisions to Alternative B, the proposed action, were made as a result of the public comments on the Draft Revised Refuge Plan. A number of technical corrections were made in response to comments and many of the editorial suggestions provided by the state of Alaska were adopted.

Alternative B, the preferred alternative, provides a realistic balance between public use of the Refuge and the conservation needs of the Refuge. Alternative B best accomplishes refuge purposes, best helps achieve the missions of the National Wildlife Refuge System and the Service, and best meets the vision and goals identified in the plan. It provides long-term protection of fish and wildlife populations and their habitats while allowing for appropriate levels of fish and wildlife-dependent recreation, interpretation and environmental education, subsistence, and other public uses.

Analysis of Impacts

The EA analyzed direct, indirect, and cumulative impacts on the physical, biological and socio-economic environment. It included an ANILCA Section 810 subsistence evaluation and finds the proposed action would not result in restrictions of subsistence use. No significant effects were identified in the analysis.

Conclusions

Based on review and evaluation of the information contained in the EA and revised plan, I have determined that there will be no significant individual or cumulative impacts to the human environment, within the meaning of section 102(2)(c) of the National Environmental Policy Act of 1969, as amended. I have determined that the activities prescribed in this plan are not major Federal actions. Accordingly, the Service is not required to prepare an environmental impact statement.

_____/Signed by/ Geoffrey L. Haskett_____   _____April 27, 2009_____

        Geoffrey L. Haskett   Date

        Regional Director

U.S. Department of the Interior
U.S. Fish & Wildlife Service

http://www.fws.gov

September 2009

Requests for additional information about the Koyukuk/Nowitna
Refuge and its Revised Comprehensive Conservation Plan should be
directed to:

Refuge Manager
Koyukuk/Nowitna National Wildlife Refuge Complex
P.O. Box 287
Galena, AK 99741

Headquarters Phone: 907-656-1231
Headquarters Fax: 907-656-1708

E-mail: r7kynwr@fws.gov

Internet: http://koyukuk.fws.gov
            http://nowitna.fws.gov

Requests for a CD-ROM or paper copy of the Revised
Comprehensive Conservation Plan for the Koyukuk/Nowitna Refuge
Complex should be directed to the Refuge at the address above or to:

U.S. Fish and Wildlife Service
Division of Conservation Planning & Policy
1011 E. Tudor Road, MS-231
Anchorage, AK 99503

Division phone: 907-786-3357
Division Fax: 907-786-3965

E-mail: koyukuknowitna_planning@fws.gov

Internet: http://alaska.fws.gov/nwr/planning/koynowpol.htm